STREAM UNDER FLIGHT

Stream under Flight

John Livingstone Clark

THISTLEDOWN PRESS

© John Livingstone Clark, 1999
All rights reserved

No part of this publication may be reproduced or transmitted in any form or by any means, graphic, electronic or mechanical, including photocopying, recording, or any information storage and retrieval system, without permission in writing from the publisher. Requests for photocopying of any part of this book shall be directed in writing to CanCopy.

Canadian Cataloguing in Publication Data

Clark, R.J. (Ronald John), 1950–
Stream under flight
Poems.
ISBN 1-895449-89-8
I. Title.
PS8555.L37185 S86 1999   C811'.54   C99-920045-3
PR9199.3.C5233 S86 1999

Cover painting by Miranda Jones
Inside drawings by J. Forrie
Typeset by Thistledown Press Ltd.
Printed and bound in Canada

Thistledown Press Ltd.
633 Main Street
Saskatoon, Saskatchewan
S7H 0J8

ACKNOWLEDGEMENTS
The author would like to thank the Saskatchewan Arts Board and the Writers' Trust for their generous support in the development of this work.

 Saskatchewan Arts Board

 The Canada Council | Le Conseil des Arts
for the Arts | du Canada
since 1957 | depuis 1957

 Canadian Heritage   Patrimoine canadien

Thistledown Press gratefully acknowledges the financial assistance of the Canada Council for the Arts, the Saskatchewan Arts Board, and the Government of Canada through the Book Publishing Industry Development Program for its publishing program.

for Anne Szumigalski
who clears the way

Contents

Section One 1-12	11
Section Two 13 - 27	24
Section Three 28 - 46	40
Section Four 47 - 51	60
Section Five 52 - 62	66
Section Six 63 - 77	78
Epilogue	93

SECTION ONE

1.

your old man left nothing. drunk, whoremonger, he left you zip. but quietly you persevere. swish-swish, your wife paints the crib; chit-chitter-chat, your small boy talks to the swallows out back. two nests under eaves full of hungry young. the old gal next door says they're good luck, so maybe three broods next year for your tow-headed son to amuse. meanwhile, on a porch facing south, you sit with cigar, pen and paper. lilacs fill your world with a different kind of poem, meadow larks polish the stillness with song. who needs the approval of others? no one need knock at your door. though farmers still wave as they saunter along—and Hutterites in black—down the narrow dirt road.

2.

you say four walls and a roof are more than enough. surrounded by elms and tall ragged spruce, your summers are filled with the flight of birds—swallows and larks, warblers, hawks. even bats at night silently swooping for bugs, a sea of wind roaring in the branches. while two miles east under endless sky, a lake full of fish hungry for hooks. who needs those books piled by your bed? words read today are but shadows tomorrow. take your son fishing—throw most of it back—then look to the hills with their plump saskatoons.

3.

butterflies in sunlight, moths at night. the mercury vapor lamp a siren for bugs, stuck to the screen like petals. in the morning you sweep them down while a few fat spiders perch quietly on the porch. but then everything odd is beautiful: like the woman who comes to tea and to argue. her hair black silk, her heart set deep in a silver cocoon. no one tastes her luminous beauty: all her rings turned to secrets on a chain around her neck; all her smiles filled with stillness, the courage of the chaste.

STREAM UNDER FLIGHT

4.

above the caraganas a meadowlark sings, yellow blossoms dripping with rain. a young woman—stone faced—dances in the yard. never does she tire of moving her limbs, this daughter, this eldest child. even soaked to the bone, she turns from your offer of simple warmth. loving her so much, this is hard to get beyond, and you pray for an end to her painful doubt. but she'll find her way out, never fear; you just crush with your love and make people weep. every step too heavy for flight.

5.

this is my real home, the dark haired woman said, a place where no mountain—no unwelcome suitor—ever sits on my mind. living here so long, she continued, I feel sky on my breast like a lover from afar: nameless heart, voiceless mind. well, you replied, grabbing her waist, I've a mind to be drunk! here's a blanket so big we could journey for days, finding our way forward and back. hands off, she slapped then quickly laughed, there's nothing so big as my hunger for peace.

6.

for fifteen years you've argued with that gal. now smarter than ever, she's also thicker at waist and hips. but you, too, show your age: breathless, stout, weary at the thought of waltzing when life comes knocking, you feign disease. though such a nice face, your dark lover croons trying to tie your shoes. so what fades faster than blossoms? you think, recalling a union long ago: small white porch, cherry petals in spring. gone like a dream that other wife, those precious kids. a lump in your throat and trembling hands. shoes untied with the memory.

7.

not much more than twenty, young Rempel goes about like he owns the place. cowboy slim with jet hair and beard, every gal with an itch soon learns his name. in winter his snowmobile roars; come summer he'll raise dust with that corvette oughta hell. who is that guy? the Hutterites ask. so blessed with life, so self-assured, he's deep in the world and won't step aside. poor lead-footed bastard—speeding through fields he'll never climb the wind.

8.

west of town lives old man Fast. with a yard jammed with Fords and bright red tractors—a hidden bar full of premier Scotch—he's the richest guy down your way. sure, when he dies, the locals will all go to his funeral. where else will you find such a perfect feast? but few real tears will ever be shed. a widow or two he might have laid; a small limping boy with an ugly dog. no, his skidoos will be stacked like old dusty toys. his wife cruising south in that cherry red Lincoln.

9.

no one's laughing here now, with books piled high to the ceiling, and rough drafts tossed on a dusty floor. soon it'll be thirty below and you'll have nothing to burn but your poems. what is it makes you scribble, you and those other earnest souls? fame among a fist full of people is no fame at all. still you dream of readers as you feed the cat kibble. dancing past a stove you find the mindful way: a widening grin as your eyes fill with dawn. even poor, it's looking rosy.

10.

think of all those beauties you've painfully adored. how many still alive? how many yet on their feet? yes, those curtains parted long ago, that silken shimmer of earthly grace: emerald eyes, moist red lips, satin skin under motel neon. thirty hard years down a crooked road and we're all boot leather. no lilac scent, no silver tinsel, no scented scarves can hide this passing.

11.

today let's toast Sylvia. lips like tender wishes, hands like eager dreams; you loved her well in your own fashion, but she never shut up in bed. for years you couldn't sleep! now she's gone to the bone yard—silenced by her own sad will. when you tasted her, though, there was joy enough for two, and spasms clapped your ears and rang away the pain. today who's left to remember that warmth? a silk shirt thrown carelessly—her mouth so alive at your breast.

12.

in a few short years where will you be? where on earth will you find your children? nothing that grows endures for long, nothing alive takes its sweet time dying. like sunny canola gone in one season, or big trees trembling at Dutch elm bugs. so where are the bairns who rode slippers through your house? laughing it up somewhere as you brood counting aches, your tortoise-shell cat hunting marbles on the floor. one daughter, two sons, and the spell of yearning: it's all you've ever learned of letting go. flying after that cat—pursuing your loves to the open.

Section Two

13.

two doors east, a woman with raven hair. once you were lovers and shared a bed. once you were friends enjoying a home. now you're apart and share the same soul. yet morning till dusk you trade stones and aspersions: "get your dog shit off my lawn!"; "get your grass off my dog's shit!" back and forth like myna birds, the laughter's infectious—so you'd think. but not many see the depth of this love, and the locals say you're mad. two old shoes crossing a stream. two bright stars in blossom.

14.

out here you're "professor". out here in the shadow of garbage mountain, you almost pass for a prominent man. but in the city— behind your back—they call you bum, uncouth, a man of fetters. who lives well in the eyes of others? who goes far without tripping a few times? not everyone with a hat can get ahead in this world. forget the predators, remember the lamb. or better yet, those black cows grazing. the golden stubble rising to meet their patient lips.

15.

hah! hustling for bucks has worn you out. buying your own books you can't sell them anywhere. so you get a discount. poetry has led you a merry chase. a shack with more holes than a colander; elms full of bats and leafless branches. how do you stay both fat and poor? the only ones to share your table are other bards: half of them crazy, none of them rich. how quickly they gobble up pots of macaroni; how swiftly they suck back your watered wine. passed out on the floor— dead to the muse—at least they block those wicked drafts.

16.

you're not stupid, you just can't get ahead. people borrow ideas but never return the favour. what use is all that learning, those dusty books? job interviews are like migratory flights, you sail through the sky until someone brings you down. who can see those guns behind the cunning willow blinds? still, you don't give up—your clothes always pressed and ready. that blue shirt covered with pelicans and carp. the tie with a pond beneath rosy clouds. who can know the ways of Fate? not every hunter has the gift of an eye.

17.

you've been abused, yet you still abuse others. where will it end? this emptiness drives most people mad, and there you go roaring like a lion. flailing about with keen words and lawsuits, muscled threats and foreclosures. god, it's a circus! and what's left when day is done? a bruise or two from the bar, popcorn in your briefs? try a passionate stillness cold as a mirror. don't kid yourself—this world's gone before you even lace your shoes.

18.

you're not the only one in tears tonight. this town full of widows and welfare mothers, old men dying and families going broke. how many trucks with for sale signs? how many boats and trailers? but no one so poor as a poet, eh? and who's to blame? that old man said to leave those tomes alone: "learn a trade, get your papers! no poem's gonna warm your bones in winter!" now wanting a stitch of dignity, you've no white Stetson to wear to the bar.

19.

a sorehead runs the only shop in town, but where else can you go for rice and fish? no matter how deep your curtsy, he always scowls then gripes about business. lovely weather, isn't it? good day for skiing? or working in the garden? but still no smile. good day for blight, you growl under your breath, then quickly take it back. who knows what stones have been placed in his heart. a nice day for smiling, you say with a grin. then exit posthaste.

20.

so where's Sophia in such an age? traffic jam jalopies spewing fumes, drecked out halls on lily fields—even towers of ivory with dirty panes. where on earth can she lay her head? a touch like the joy of budding dreams, her golden body like warmest silk. you've given it all to court this girl: poetry stitched with worn rags; a few hundred words gathered in silence.

21.

you slave in vain on the latest theory: endless hours on footnotes in French. while in malls of academe your cane is a joke, all the students on skateboards with laptop brains. in this world, age has become the only monster—stumbling through night with a body made of death. who sees the ripening of heart in mind? gold fields under a pelican sky; rowan limbs full of azure and birds. every year still younger where it counts.

22.

by the old town hall, a sheen of roses. palominos at sunset like something other, tails and manes now candles aflame. but these mares—sweet maidens in thick green grass—only have eyes for ribbons and boys. so you circle the field with a metal detector, lost change going for coffee or beer. and silence fills dusk like water from a stream. your mind and beard aquiver with joy.

23.

libraries have followed you everywhere. granddad's from Victoria, now your father's from Prince George. thirty years gathering books, now it's all computers and the net. "web sites are for spiders," you mumble, stacking, restacking your restless tomes ."when the power goes out a flame still shows the way!" brave talk, though it doesn't pay the bills. who needs words to rest in a field? at the edge of the sky, a mind flies home in silence.

24.

once young and green eyed—with thick curly hair—you came to know bliss in the art of love. now all those lovers are dead or in sales. who can ever tell where fragrant thighs lead? and when feral cats yowl under shady elms, how happy you are to be old and deaf: this passage through silence so tough on the balls. yes glad enough now with those tokens of desire—so relieved to know they're just tokens.

25.

Fritz Perls couldn't do it out Cowichan Valley—not Jung on a scroll or Bubba Ram Das. acid didn't do it or magic morels. not love, lust, or a blend of both: sweet lips and fingers on a carousal. no words come close, though poetry comes near: golden sunlight through a stand of red cedar, dust motes dancing on heavy green boughs. silence a way, but never the goal. it calls even now— this stream under flight.

26.

sure, you've seen the world. from Sydney to Edinburgh, from Snowden to Tamalpais. loving views you've sat on peaks; loving oceans you've crossed the widest. full moon strolls down Bondi beach, a gal on your arm in lavender silk. two crones on Skye, a third in Kitsilano—the cards always pointing somewhere else. now years on the prairies tending your trees; piling bales of hay against cold winter walls. death nothing to fear—life nothing to cling to. though who on the coast could have seen you here? a Salt Spring Island boy knocking frost off willows, trudging with a whistle down a frozen road.

27.

born out west fifty years ago, then myriad miles on winding roads. where are the rivers full of sharks and bears, those oaken meadows older than saints? you've studied hard in contemplation; expanded your mind, tried every quack. always searching for the realm of the real, you've never once dreamt of drifting snow—of pearl grey skies and scrubby windbreaks, brown leaves twitching in a frosty breeze. so when your furnace shuts down, the silence is complete. cats in the willows looking for cover.

SECTION THREE

28.

your shack's on the edge of a working field, but you don't work the garden much anymore. a few herbs and onions, a hill of spuds. the rest gone to hell and purple loosestrife. meanwhile—on the highway south—crows feast daily on some poor creature's fate. is man just a crow with occasional manners? appetite is appetite: beaks and teeth. yet how quiet you've become amidst elms and spruce, muttering over a bowl of cold rice, slumbering with pen and empty paper. maybe there is a way: the rise and fall of a single breath; the end of a line where something blossoms.

29.

with only bees and crickets, endless skies and ranks of clouds, you sit for days—nothing in mind. preferring cool breezes, you walk the fields at dusk and dawn. from under shady elms and scrubby spruce, your musings rise over refuse peak. but up the road's a woman who can't live without lucre. like a sorry magpie, she shatters the peace: this cost, that price, what she'll inherit. how happy you are when they cut off your phone, how quiet your dreams under garbage mountain—of pelicans lifting over the sky.

STREAM UNDER FLIGHT

30.

clothes and belly fit only for the sticks, you shun Broadway lights and the chic West End. besides, who goes to tailors these days? though your father and the loggers dressed well in the forties. so, no crease or pleats in your pants looking sharp—no classy fabric to breath in and out. just cheap stretchy stuff dusty and worn. Szumigalski in the pocket of your coat full of holes; Han Shan stuffed deep in an old leather bag. a few bucks for the road and look who's under way—ball cap adorned with wings and fins.

31.

wanting to stroll into the city, you had your boots resoled then cut a stout walking stick. how pretty those weeds in summer along the tracks—rushes in the ditches, willows bending in a breeze. but you never got past the nearest field. summer golden, winter white: always a border for the azure beyond. in the spell of the distance, the walk can wait. soon comes lilac and a scent from the hedges.

32.

living in the country has gone to your head. a pile of publications makes you some kind of wheel. besides, half the locals are built like you. bears in baggy sweat suits, Holsteins in halter tops. but when you go to the coast it's another matter: your belly precedes you and the jokes are endless. where have all your dad's friends gone? the fishermen and loggers, the truck drivers and cops? what on earth have they done with that girth? it's not on the sea-wall around Stanley Park, with its weight limit for joggers and dress code for the beach. old bodies—old anchors—rusting in brine.

33.

who can keep lilacs in bloom for long? though the smell of them works on your mind all year. you crawl full length into six foot hedges, just to come close to their scent of heaven. and today, picking blossoms, your face drops thirty years. nothing good can be kept forever. nothing good ever ends.

STREAM UNDER FLIGHT

34.

glancing east to trash mountain—ripe like a pimple on the fair skinned prairie—you see an eyesore rise between earth and sky. who will ever fathom the industry of men? but willow and aspen skirt the lake at its feet, graceful, slender through all the seasons. and trout, pickerel, whitefish, jack: they brighten twilight with sleek silver backs. the thought of fish is much on your mind, as clouds with cowls peer through windows. they murmur "empty hands, drop your fists." receive in silence what can be given.

35.

blooming lilacs take you home to Salt Spring, those various perfumes out in the bush. when elms turn orange and maples scarlet, you drift back to the hills east of Vancouver—that clamorous colour up steep wooded slopes. youth has slipped away for good, and the lists of the dead get longer every year. old bagpipe davey with his warm scottish burr; your mother-in-law, gennie, with her southern belle chimes. though trees aren't as tall here, or rivers as broad, these clouds are vaster than all the earth. honour the dead, but don't cry forever. the mind a sky full of endless promise.

36.

hopping through branches out front, that crow never strays too far from the trunk. once he might have carried books—the *tao te ching*, for example, or the *diamond sutra*—but now he's lost more than he ever learned. hungry, he eats; tired, he sleeps. who can match the sparkle in his ancient eye? who would ever think that his forked tongue would heal? truth requiring more of eye than tongue.

37.

wild roses last as long as they can, fruit trees flower then dry up fast. this land's tough on blossoms, where droughts and blizzards set the pace. but more rare still—more fragile than petals—are people with heart who wade into the stream. even poets seem mostly whiners and jerks, no time for the pen with their hands in strange pockets. yes, that wild rosy scent fills spring with wonder. in a moment's breath—standing still, you kill time.

38.

that writer up the tracks you sometimes visit. why can't he listen or find his way home? here's a simple rule for the prairies: never travel without adequate light. even a moon can be your friend in the middle of nowhere. and how coyotes like to howl at the edge of a field. but with the moon for a lamp nothing ever seems lost.

39.

on a road to the city, people rush off to work. way east of your shack you can almost hear them cursing. yes, once you envied the fruits of their labour: big office, big car, big money. but now you've got your own work, and your hands are never still. in spring a garden for spuds and herbs—in winter you shovel snow and scatter seed for the birds. who needs a briefcase for gathering wood? deep within a breath you find real wages, while nothing of value ever turns up on the market. why not try tao jones for a lasting return?

Stream under Flight

40.

the empty prairie flows in every direction, yet winter or summer its size is a constant. how long does it take to reckon the infinite? black skies shrink the world, blue skies open. why be chained to moods and arbitrary colours? things just come and go on this endless plain; all is aflux and nothing lasts. so why remain a figure when you're also the ground?

41.

what would be said if they could see you now? this ragged lawn with dusty white spruce. this shack turned south towards empty fields, walls more holey than a christmas manger. sensing each day present breathing on its own, you tramp the yard doing odd little jobs. then out by the wood pile, time holds its breath—the floating world now naked and true. watering seedlings, counting birds, this is where your roots are found. laughing at that ski hill with its trashy heart.

42.

cold prairie is full of wierd sights, like the guy whose hat was a small golden cocker. "damn coyotes got him two winters ago," he mutters, "but I still like to walk him now and then." chairs made from milkcans and tractor seats, rough Buddhist altars in behind barns, a matron in the bar with a pig on leash. but the stars are brighter here, and closer than plums on old stooped trees. the air, when it rains, like alfalfa honey—a gift from bees and summer fields. a gift to those who never leave.

43.

self-pity's like throwing mud on a mirror: so much for reflection. and how quickly days flow like sand through your fingers. how quickly they fly like swallows in august. in one short life there's barely time to smile, or to learn how to bow artlessly. say yes to it all while your tongue still moves—don't waste time on frowns and woe. your ashes can sleep for eternity.

44.

last night in dream you returned to the coast. up to her elbows in contracts and flyers, your ex-wife was busy. buying/selling, her pen never stopped. but even with her face on signs all over, she's still not sure who she really is. and when you murmured her name, she paused only for a moment. "and who are you?" her blank eyes queried. too many years down two different paths—now your belly hangs low and your beard's streaked grey. time only heals by taking away. why reach for the past when you breathe in the present?

45.

sure there's a road to your ratty shack. but don't look for pavement to the centre of the heart. cold mountain, cold prairie—call it what you will. every tree in your yard with different branches; every human soul with a different journey. just reach like those poplars and stretch for the sun. put roots in the ground and be on your way.

46.

let's drop all this crap about who knows what—when the lord's coming back, who's damned or saved. why not just agree that the mystery's getting deeper. that wise folks sleep well knowing nothing at all. so tend to your carrots and columbine; learn to brew tea, be kind to kids. the breath rises and falls like a ship at sea. the mind unfurled—well into the stream.

SECTION FOUR

47.

they talk of a tree older than history, back to the days when this was all bush. roots curling down to an ancient sea bed, its leaves over time have touched myriad lives. speechless, it's been called the bole of truth—in stillness it's listened to a hundred different tongues. now most only see that blackened bark, the lightening scars of its riven trunk. but its aged core is a diamond grain; free of attention, it's rooted in flight.

48.

your body may once have seemed a temple, but now it's more of a flop house or jail. all your precious time's spent attending to wants. no wonder you never get out of the house—always filling your face or emptying bowels. even birds spend more time flying than shitting. what will you have to show for your life? worn out teeth and a tired ass? you and those poets scrounging drinks and meals. silence the one true leaven.

49.

living far from family, no wonder you get down. your kids on the coast don't call anymore, all grown up with woes of their own. only an empty grave remembers your name: St. Mary's Anglican, Fulford Harbour. so what have you sought over the years? nothing that flies on the wings of words. but discern the shimmer between silver birch—or out beyond the golden fields—then the mind will suddenly rest a spell. having finally learned the value of nothing.

50.

put those feet in your mouth as much as you want, you can't step twice in the same old stream. isn't that how the wisdom goes? so why cling so much to honeyed flesh? fucking's fine, just don't get hooked. when your big bones are crumbling under the turf, don't bother with that wake up call. take the time now to breathe in a pool of quiet. one candle in the dark, feel the soft inner touch.

51.

who are those mandarins in their academic robes? at nightfall they stumble from post to post. no lucent eyes, no loving heart; it's all "I, I, I" with that mean bunch. you trust the soul, seeing things unseen. don't worry about pants that wrestle with your belly. enjoy this shack on the edge of a field—relish your view of garbage mountain. singing to the sun, kissing the rain—it might never get better than this.

SECTION FIVE

Stream under Flight

52.

elevators engorged along grid roads and tracks? yes, crops are in—a year's work in the bin—and local folks ready to head for the sun. Arizona, Mexico, Florida, Cuba: anywhere there's no snow and ice. and you stand on the highway going south, plywood sign reading "poet seeks patron." you remain in the wind for a very long time, feet and beard frozen from that northern blast. a man in rags with ink on his lips—those fifth wheelers have no space for you. so back to your shack and a prayer to the muse. on the wings of a poem, your galoshes take flight.

53.

the shack where you'll die is not on a map. in summer you bake like a trout in the dirt, a few last gasps under the fire. in winter your teeth chatter prayers for the kids—a place too far for visits. but it's just right for vistas, so crying time is over. whether hot or cold, dark or light, something in mind has woven together. embracing the field, you ramble south—sun rise can occur any time of the day.

54.

doing everything you were told—mastering the art of pleasing others—look where you've landed. this drafty shack in a cold hard land, no leaves on the trees six months of the year. and that honking last night, that drunken wake: geese flying south with all the ponds frozen. so why waste the time left in your flask? take a cue from that field across the path. in august it blooms green and gold—but in winter it's quiet with nothing in mind.

55.

hoar frost on branches as you walk along, hitchhiking south and out of the city. down to your place by the Hutterite field. rich men in Lincolns swing by without a care, thinking, "another old man with too many stories." poverty like dogshit, it sticks to your boots. and they don't want that stink on their limousine mats. ah, compassion à la mode—thank god for the Schwan man. though now you'll have to buy some of his fare; ice cream to go with a frozen world.

56.

magpies outside the door at dawn, though old storm windows deaden their chatter. music in your eyes as red berries sparkle; branches full of waxwings eating their fill; that slender pink rowan arousing winter. who deserves these hues around your shack? who'd think so little could be so so much? trees full of rubies, purple stoles in the sky—your eyes see thrones wherever they rest.

57.

who could ever toss such a loyal friend? alone in a room overlooking the fields, your bed is a lover with broken springs. in summer you awake to a hundred birds, come winter the trees pass secrets through the blinds—dead leaf silhouettes dancing on the breeze. in dream you return to a life on the coast, from Campbell River to Monterey. but who knows what counts when you're buried in the world? let silence bring us back to zero. in that shadow of desire something new comes to mind.

58.

out here coyotes cry all summer, and the dogs in town howl back at night. if not for those fools on snowmobiles, silence would rule the winter. no wiser than swallows, they zigzag the prairie then head for a bar: that welcoming world of cigars and whisky. but the cold plains you cross are safe from intrusion. no noisy toys will venture out here—those empty fields that open within.

59.

the summer sun blisters the side of your shack, while in winter cold knives slice the crummy walls. but insulation's cheap—like fine pink hair in an old man's ears, suddenly it appears in every crack. but to hell with comfort. the view from one window's the price of a palace: silver willows against the sky, fields and dirt roads that go on forever. every day there's silence and passage for the sun. every moment filled with some kind of light.

60.

this month the snow is late, but poets still hunker down in town. cars not fit for winter drives, shoes not fit for walking to the bus. so the Hutterite field is your only friend, through all four seasons it makes you smile. but off to the east that landfill tumor—that trashy alp for people with cash. strapping on skis they mount the slopes, haughty laughter stinging the night. but you've still got wine and ambrosial words: Han Shan at daybreak, Rilke at dusk. even the berries fermenting come from these plains— growth in the open like a wine-filled song.

61.

in the beginning, god voided, lit the gas, then set down critters on a small nub of clay. you don't really know much about god, but on long winter nights you'll cry out for solace. then come spring we'll see you dancing at dawn, praising misty mornings and those pelicans overhead. whatever's going on it doesn't make much sense. let's just hope it doesn't count on you—the only way out's through the open.

62.

on the edge of this field, you could write a good story with only four words. it would open and close with, "I am not here." leaving much time for shovelling snow, for feeding crows and chickadees— leaving days and nights for breathing in silence. in the face of trash mountain, it's enough of a plot.

Section Six

63.

the road to your shack is the one ploughs forget, no tire tracks ever rutting the snow. just waxwings and chickadees flitting through the trees—a neighbour's pigeons, some skunks on the ground. everything's closed and the rats in those granaries remember fatter times. but who has better trees? all the yards overgrown with aspen and spruce. folks move on but trees keep the centre. what is there really to chase anymore? at the end of the road abandon your car. each step a breath, each breath a journey.

64.

if you're looking for a place to rest your mind, forget the Rockies or those western isles. tourists flock there like gulls at a dump, and the clink of silver is louder than hell. why not seek the humblest place—buy a shack and sit still on the edge of a field. no one gets tanned like the coyotes here, no one eats better than the ducks and crows. and all year long birds visit from afar: goldfinches, orioles, meadowlarks, geese. even lofty pelicans on their way up north. after years of handshakes—the honesty of wings.

65.

you think too much of the old days. strong of body and will, you raged with the gang from S.F.U.—like across to those islands to squat on beaches. huddled down on Hornby, strung out in Tofino, the sensual risks of foggy cedar groves. then riding the rods from Smithers to George, hiding in railyards with ferns in caps. a few tabs in your wallet, Rimbaud in a bag—it seemed like the seers were set to wake up. those freaks in back of a rusty pickup, down the Fraser Canyon, burnt faces to the sun. you're better here now with deer in the willows—a silent stream full of golden carp.

66.

if they came with offers of big dough now, what would you say? piffle? piss off? too late for this kingdom's keys? a solo magpie in the lattice of elms, tail feathers flashing in the bitter wind: what raucous cries of arcane lore. why go elsewhere when the answer's before you? nothing with a pricetag has anything to teach. sift through the garbage for the pearls that smile.

Stream under Flight

67.

the plains stretch farther than eyes can see, and in winter the snow is a provisional sea: water over earth, air over water, fire in the sky, in the humble hearth. who cares if the snowplough's sometimes late? you're not going anywhere in the world that matters. porridge on the shelf and water in the tank; enough wood for months to heat your shack. so let cold roads vanish and bright ways open. dwelling in quiet—a living stone in the stream.

68.

"those books won't save you," says the hunter next door. "writing poems won't keep you out of the grave. so why bother with words and rhymes at all?" just think for a moment of a winter forest, cold as hell and full of horror: like wolves frozen stiff with their teeth in a buck. on each tree a letter, in, each corpse a line. yes, there's life in the search for a perfect phrase. sink your fangs in a poem— see if it bleeds.

Stream under Flight

69.

five months of the year you freeze your ass, then it's hot cross buns for another four. in the cracks in between are found young green blades, sweet red berries, a crocus or two. expect nothing here but sky, for the only peaks you'll find are the ones in your head. keep breathing, keep counting, keep kneeling and still. embrace silence like a lover to the heat of your loins. then your days will fall like leaves from a tree that never dies.

70.

from atop trash mountain the prairie falls away: light snow and stubble, thickets of willow, birch, aspen, manitoba maple at your feet a long lake full of trout and pike. to the north a small city of gamy passions. then tiny hamlets west and south, with bright painted shacks for old folks and bums. dawn lends its light: saffron and rose. just breathe with your eyes whenever you can—seeing is all that really matters.

STREAM UNDER FLIGHT

71.

you only came out for part-time work, but never got back to the coast. who would have reasoned that winter would claim you? fifteen years at the end of this summer. but a season below zero is just another meditation—so easy to count breaths when they turn to ice. even hearts beat slower like the earth in winter, and minds find themselves with nothing to do. why envy the rich with their speedboats and yachts? no one so encumbered ever finds the stream.

72.

you'll shed a few tears going west this summer. everyone you loved has died or disappeared. old couples splitting, kids gone with the flow—they sink below the surface only phoning for cash. where are your blood kin? the ex-wives and lovers? at least that grave at Fulford will remind them you lived—half a plot for ashes and poems. close to cedars and wild roses.

73.

in your shack a grotto, but within that nothing. what a paradox, heh? so much rising from so much nothing. a gleam like stars at the centre of your dwelling. now a few beets or spuds can feed the body, a blanket or poncho keep it warm. but let the lords of the land draw nigh this secret. a presence of light, an absence of shadow.

74.

tonight trash mountain's lit up like a circus. night skiers, snow boarders, booze and dope. slap and tickle hot tubs, fun while it lasts. recalling that heat, you feel your balls tingle. but then a platinum moon slips out of the fog, Orion's diamonds strewn over black silk. a frost on the rowans, tinsel on the pines, how fast the body cools in the early winter night. how far your mind reaches in the wake of desire.

75.

some say drugs or brain damage at birth—whatever the case you're ever unruly. others pile profits or work on their bodies, but you make war on the solemn and formal. always good for a joke, you're unattached at last—a fool for the dawn and heavy as a bear. who says wisdom has to hurt? with chuckles and farts, striking matches for truth, you're light where it counts, at the end of day. humouring the dark with lamplit eyes.

76.

you'd give a monk the shirt off your back, and a drunk your last bowl of rice. why get stuck on the things of this world when the only way out's through the eye of a . . . noodle? life is a gift so pass it around—and don't sit doodling till your skull's in the weeds, no one gets more than the giver. harbingers of death, these tough stingy hearts. barren lives on the banks of the stream.

Stream under Flight

77.

so many friends gone, old and young: all in the ground with no need for breath. but dawn hits the rime and a wide world explodes, light pointillistic falling from trees. and that shadow with hat just out beyond the elms? an old trucker with a dog trying to heal, his hours all stolen by nameless fear. but now silence, the field, gathers him in, tears quickly turning to pins of brightness. no answers, no words, no two cents worth— just a turn in the mind, this stream under flight.

Epilogue

After words? Silence. And before words and in between words? Silence. And when all the words of all peoples, cultures, times, species, places—even planets—when all those breathy morphemes and phonemes have fallen into the dust. When every name ever named is unbound from the web of accidents and qualifications. Then? Silence. That great begetter of mysteries, of demigods, inquiries, postulations, anxieties, and rebirths. That great fount of poetry and knowledge, for as Apollonius of Tyana said silence is also a *logos*.

Alone for the first time in over fifteen years, I had recently moved to a small town south of Saskatoon—a humble house on the edge of vast rolling fields. And there, particularly during my first winter, I was thrown once again into the vast cauldron of silence. Staring past my computer—through the front windows and out across the empty white horizon—I found myself being emptied out by forces seemingly outside the sway of human constructions, particularly language. It threw me back to my studies in Eastern Religion almost three decades earlier, and I ran to Lao-tzu and the others with both hunger and pleasure: "The *tao* that can be told is not the eternal *tao*; the name that can be named is not a permanent name." Or in the words of the Buddha, "There is, O monks, an Unborn, Unoriginated, Uncreated, Unformed. If there were not this Unborn, this Unorginated, this Uncreated, this Unformed, escape from the world of the born, the originated, the created, the formed, would not be possible."

And so I came to Han Shan's *Cold Mountain* poems, and a creative response to my new life situation seemed not only possible but imperative. His Cold Mountain is my—is our—cold prairie, and so this work evolved. Pursuing silence further into nothingness, like one of Rilke's "bees of the invisible", yet at the same time remaining faithful to the social world around me and hopefully eschewing any clichés of the mysterious East. "While alive/Be a dead man," D.T. Suzuki once said, but the silence of such dying always leads to new life. Where better for poems to begin?

Dundurn, SK, March 1999